Produced by JaDon Management Inc.
1405 4th Ave. N. W. #109
Ardmore, Ok. 73401

ISBN:
978-1-937501-00-6

Cover Design by:
Jeffrey T. McCormack
Apologia Book Shoppe
www.apologiabooks.com

IN FLAMING FIRE!
A REVEALING LOOK AT THE REVELATION OF CHRIST
Don K. Preston D. Div.

Years ago, there was a book entitled *The Day Christ Came* written by a popular minister, David Roper. The book gave a dramatic presentation of the coming of Christ. In my early ministry I would use that book as a sermon, reading it with emphasis and passion. Very often, the audience would be in tears as the story of open graves, cosmic destruction and lost souls unfolded. That work was based on 2 Thessalonians 1:4f.

From my youth, sitting at the feet of many "famous" preachers, I have heard this text quoted as proof and description of the end of time. Here is what the passage says.

"and to give you who are troubled rest with us when the Lord Jesus is revealed from heaven with His mighty angels, in flaming fire taking vengeance on those who do not know God, and on those who do not obey the gospel of our Lord Jesus Christ. These shall be punished with everlasting destruction from the presence of the Lord and from the glory of His power, when He comes, in that Day, to be glorified in His saints and to be admired among all those who believe, because our testimony among you was believed." (NKJV)

Wow! What an incredible passage! What an impressive prediction. Pretty scary too. It is all about the end of time, right? It predicts the visible descent of Christ out of heaven, at some point in the future, right? Well, actually, believe it or not, there is a very real problem with applying this incredible prophecy to a yet future, literal coming of Christ at the end of time. Now, that might shock you at first, but, I hope that you will stay with me as we take a revealing look at the revelation of Jesus Christ.

I will never forget my very first day of seminary class on 2 Thessalonians. The professor began by candidly saying: "Gentlemen, I must confess to you that I have a problem with 2 Thessalonians 1." Someone asked what problem he had. He responded that on a simple straightforward reading of the text, that it clearly indicated that the Thessalonians were currently being persecuted and that Paul was promising that Christ was going to give them relief from that persecution at his coming. Of course, he *knew* that Christ did not come and give them that promised relief, and *that was the problem*. He did not know how to resolve the problem that Paul made a prediction that did not come true.

Another problem he had, and this did raise my eyebrows at the time, was the fact that in the great majority of sermons based on this text, the quotation almost invariably begins with verse 7 and does not include the foregoing context. He pondered whether we would use the text as much if we were to actually honor the *context*.

When he read the previous verses, the class squirmed uncomfortably for a moment, for we could see the professor's point. Nonetheless, by and large, most of us, myself included, simply dismissed the "problem." After all, this was one of the most commonly used passages to preach from to get folks walking down the aisle. It is dramatic, it is compelling, it is powerful! We could hardly accept such a challenge to our thinking at the time and since the professor had no logical explanation, we just "moved on" in our discussion. That was the end of *that*, until I began later to truly pay attention to the entire context of the passage. *Then* I realized, *fully*, that the professor was *right*.

I discovered that when you read all of the context that 2 Thessalonians 1 does pose a huge threat to a belief in a future coming of the Lord. I discovered that I was personally guilty of misapplying the text. I discovered that the proper rules of hermeneutic (that is the science of proper interpretation) have to be ignored or distorted in order to make the passage apply to your future and mine.

Maybe it will help to present the previous verses for you to read. Then, we will point out the things that troubled our professor and those things that have led me to the thoughts presented herein.

"We ourselves boast of you among the churches of God for your patience and faith in all your persecutions and tribulations that you endure, which is manifest evidence of the righteous judgment of God, that you may be counted worthy of the kingdom of God, for which you also suffer; since it is a righteous thing with God to repay with tribulation those who trouble you, and to give you who are troubled rest with us when the Lord Jesus is revealed from heaven with His mighty angels, in flaming fire taking vengeance on those who do not know God, and on those who do not obey the gospel of our Lord Jesus Christ. These shall be punished with everlasting destruction from the presence of the Lord and from the glory of His power, when He comes, in that Day, to be glorified in His saints and to be admired among all those who believe, because our testimony among you was believed."

Here is what I would like to ask you to do. I would like you to remember the basic rules of journalism, the basic rules of *hermeneutic*, as you consider these verses again. Those rules are:

Who? Who is writing, who is he writing *to*, who is he writing *about*? Paul the apostle wrote the epistle. He wrote *to*, "the church of the Thessalonians" (2 Thessalonians 1:1). He wrote *about* those persecuting the Thessalonians. Pretty simple and clear, right?

What? *What does Paul say?* Answer: he is writing to tell them that he is aware of their faith *and their suffering* and is offering them hope in the midst of *that suffering (v. 4)*. He told them that they were going to get *relief* from their persecution and suffering (v. 7). We will develop this later.

When? *When was he writing* and *when does he apply his writings*? Paul was writing in the first century. No problem there. However, the next question begins to raise some issues. *When did Paul say that the Thessalonians would receive the relief that he is promising them?* The answer is in the oft quoted verse, "When the Lord Jesus is revealed from heaven." *Now*, do you see the problem? I suspect that about now, if you have really clued into these basic questions, that you "see the train coming." So, stay with us, this will be an exciting study.

Where? Where are the events taking place, where were/are they to take place? The answer: *In the world of the Thessalonians.*

How? How does the author describe the events he describes, how will they be fulfilled, etc. Answer: the Thessalonians would be given relief from their persecution by the revelation of Christ from heaven (v. 7).

Why? Why does the author write? Why does he say what he says? Why will the events he describes, occur? Answer: Paul is clearly writing to living breathing humans to assure them that they are about to receive relief from their suffering.

What we are really talking about here is something called "audience relevance." What did the text mean to the people to whom it was written, at the time it was written, under the circumstances it was written? What we must realize, from the outset is that we are reading someone else's mail when we read the Bible. After all, if we found a letter that grandpa wrote to "gram mama" before she became grandma, and that letter said that grandpa was going to come to her house real soon, we would know, would we not, that this did not mean that grandpa had not yet come? We would know, would we not, that the specific promise given at that time, under specific circumstances, to specific individuals are not to be applied specifically to our time?

3

Does that negate the *meaning* of grandfather's letter? Does it mean that his letter has no significance for us? I think we can pretty much agree that grandfather traveling to see grandmother, while that coming was fulfilled, it most assuredly has "meaning" for us today, because without that fulfilled event, we would not even exist!

Not to be facetious but, there is not a single book of the Bible that begins with, "To the church in Ardmore, Oklahoma, in 2015!" (Interestingly, and amazingly, I had a man actually tell me that the original epistles were not intended to have meaning to the original recipients, but, to us today!)

Since I began to ask these questions and to investigate the text of 2 Thessalonians 1 more fully, I have come to realize how serious the problem of 2 Thessalonians 1 really is. I have come to realize why my professor was so troubled. Now, we have a couple of choices here. We can do our "due diligence," ask those questions and seek for solid Biblical answers to the problem, or, we can ignore the questions and the problem, and just go our merry way, not concerned with what Paul really said. Personally, though, I don't want to just keep repeating what I have heard. *I want the Truth.* And, I think that you do as well. That is why you have this book in your hands. So, what did Paul mean?

Let me warn you right now, that asking these questions and finding the answers to them is going to be a bit unsettling for you. It surely was to me. However, the writer of Proverbs says: "Buy the Truth and sell it not." Let's begin our investigation in earnest then, based on the questions we have just asked and the answers to those questions that the text gives us. We will keep things as brief as possible.

Here are the *undeniable facts* from 2 Thessalonians 1:

1.) *The Thessalonians were being persecuted for their faith in Jesus Christ.* Paul uses the present participial form (for simplicity sake, that is just the *present tense*) of the Greek word *thlipsis (meaning pressure)* four times to speak of what they were enduring (v. 4, 5, 6, 7). He also uses the present indicative of *pasxo*, which is suffering. This is undeniable. To be honest, I don't know of *anyone* that denies this. It sounds so simple and so "unthreatening" to admit that the Thessalonians were experiencing persecution. However, the fact that it was the Thessalonian church, *2000 years ago*, that was suffering is of *vital importance.*

2.) It was the Jewish community that was instigating and leading that persecution (Acts 17; 1 Thessalonians 2:15-17). This is undeniable.

4

3.) Paul promised that Christ would grant the Thessalonian church *relief* from that persecution (verse 7, "to you who are troubled, *rest*," from the Greek word *anesis*, meaning *relief from pressure*). This is undeniable.

4.) The persecutors of the Thessalonians would have the tables turned on them and they would become the persecuted ("it is a righteous thing with God to repay with tribulation (*thlipsis*) them that trouble you.") *The persecutors would become the persecuted.* This is undeniable.

5.) Now, here is where my professor saw the problem and this really is where the problem lies. The promised relief of *the Thessalonians* would be given, "when the Lord Jesus is revealed from heaven" (v. 7). This is undeniable. *Now*, do you see the train coming?

Here is the question that we have to ask even though it will probably challenge your traditional beliefs to the core, just as it did mine: *Did Jesus come, in the lifetime of the Thessalonians and give the Thessalonians relief from the persecution that they were, at that time, experiencing? Yes, or No?[1]*

If you answered, "No, Jesus did not come in the lifetime of the Thessalonians and he did not give them relief from their persecution, *this means that Paul made a false prediction.* Go back, right now if you would, and read the inspired text again, and ask yourself the basic questions one more time. Was Paul writing to the first century church at Thessalonica? *Sure he was.* Were *they* being persecuted *at that time?* Yes, they were. Did Paul promise *them* relief from that persecution? No doubt about it. Did he say that relief would come, "when the Lord Jesus is revealed from heaven?" *He most assuredly did.*

Do you see the problem clearly now? The problem is *real* and very *serious*. If you are like me, and believe in the inspiration of scripture and the Deity of Jesus, you cannot accept that Jesus' own apostle was mistaken, misguided, or wrong in his predictions. I believe Paul was inspired by the Holy Spirit to write what he did, don't you? So, how do we solve this problem?

---

[1] I have asked this question of my opponents in several formal public debates. Invariably, my opponents have answered, "No, Jesus did not come in the lifetime of the Thessalonians and give them relief from their persecution." This answer charges Paul with making a false prophecy and is a very serious issue.

If Paul was writing to living Christians, *and he was,*
And if those Christians were being persecuted, *and they were,*
And if Paul promised those living Christians relief from that persecution, *and he did,*
And if Paul promised those living Christians relief from that persecution, "when the Lord Jesus is revealed from heaven." *and he did,*
Then, if Jesus did not come in the lifetime of those living Christians and give them relief from that persecution, as promised by Paul, then, Paul lied to them, and gave them a false hope. His prediction failed, and he is guilty of being a false prophet! *That* **is the problem of the text and it is unavoidable.**

There is really no doubt about what Paul said. So, was he *wrong*? No, he wasn't. The problem is *us*. The problem is not allowing ourselves to understand the background for what Paul is saying. That is probably not our fault. We have been taught, indoctrinated if you will, to read Thessalonians through Christian eyes, and not through the eyes of Paul *proclaiming the fulfillment of Israel's last days prophecies.*[2] However, if we allow Paul to speak to us as a prophet proclaiming the imminent fulfillment of the hope of Israel, being played out in Judah's last days, then the text before us opens itself up in a marvelous way. So, with that in mind, let's take a look at 2 Thessalonians through the eyes of Paul, preacher of the hope of Israel, shall we?

---

[2] Lest it be objected that Paul was the minister to the Gentiles, which of course is true, we would note that as minister to the Gentiles, he was fulfilling God's OT promises made to Israel to bring all nations into the kingdom (Deuteronomy 32:21f; Isaiah 49:6f; 65:1f, etc.). The modern view that the Gentiles were called only because Israel rejected the kingdom and as a substitute for her is false. It was God's plan all along that national Israel would reject the gospel and the gospel go to all nations. So, Paul's ministry to the Gentiles was not a sign of the failure of God's promises, it was proof *that God's promises were being fulfilled* and that Old Covenant Israel had reached the climax of her Theocratic history.

ISAIAH 2-4: THE SOURCE OF 2 THESSALONIANS 1

To properly understand 2 Thessalonians 1, we must examine Isaiah 2-4. Why? Because as everyone will admit, *context* is the key to properly interpreting any text. And without doubt, Isaiah 2-4 is the original context, it is the fountain from whence 2 Thessalonians 1 flows. Now to some, this will seem completely strange, for many commentators *see no relationship between the passages.*[3] However, it is important to realize something right here and that is that Paul's *eschatology* (fancy word for the "end time events" of the coming of the Lord, judgment, etc.) was, according to his own words, taken directly from Moses and the prophets.[4] He says he preached *nothing* but the hope of Israel (Acts 24:14f; 25:8f; 26:6f; 28:20f). Furthermore, what escapes the notice of the majority of students is that in 2 Thessalonians 1:9 Paul quotes *verbatim*, from Isaiah 2:10, 19, 21 (He quotes from the Septuagint, the Greek translation of the Hebrew OT. *LXX* is the symbol for the *Septuagint*). So, Paul's prediction of the Day of the Lord is Isaiah's prediction of the Day of the Lord.

Isaiah 2-4 foretold that in the last days, "The Day of the Lord of Hosts shall come on everything proud and lofty"(Isaiah 2:12). In that day, "They shall go into the holes of the rocks and into the caves of the earth, *from the terror of the Lord and the glory of His majesty,* when He arises to shake the earth mightily"* (v. 10, 19, 21, my emphasis).[5] (The English translation of Isaiah is based on the Hebrew text. Paul is quoting *verbatim* from the LXX, the *Greek* translation of

---

[3] Ed Stevens and I engaged in a formal public debate in Queens, NY, in April, 2002. Our opponents were amillennialists Kevin Hartley and Gary George. In the Q and A session, I presented the connection between 2 Thessalonians 1 and Isaiah 2-4. It so shook our opponents that they simply said "No comment." Audio tapes of that debate are available from me.

[4] It is critical to understand that the NT writers repeatedly affirm that their hope of the coming of the Lord, judgment and resurrection, was "the hope of Israel," and was in fact taken directly from the OT promises made to Israel (Acts 3:21f; Acts 24:14f; 1 Peter 1:4-10; 2 Peter 3:1-2; Revelation 10:7). The idea that the doctrine of the "Second Coming" is a NT revelation concerned with the end of the Christian Age is totally misguided.

[5] Other OT predictions of the *Day of Jehovah* that Jesus applies to his coming are Zechariah 14:5 / Matthew 24:31; Joel 2:28-32/ Matthew 24:29.

7

the Hebrew. The NT writers used both the Hebrew text and the Septuagint in their quotations).

This prophecy is definitely about a historical Day of the Lord judgment on Israel. It would be a time when men could flee to the mountains from the presence of the Lord (2:10, 12, 19f). If men could escape from the Lord's coming, it is pretty clear that it is not the end of the material creation, in a moment, in the twinkling of an eye. It would be a time of famine (3:1f) when Jehovah would judge His people (3:8, 13f) in the time of "*the* war" (3:25) when, "your men shall fall by the edge of the sword" (3:25; compare Luke 21:24). This last days judgment would also be when Jehovah would remove Israel's blood guilt through judgment (4:4f). All of these events force us to conclude that Isaiah is not predicting an end of time, earth burning event. Nonetheless, he *was* predicting the Day of the Lord. It may be time to change our concepts of what the Day of the Lord really means.

Jesus came *in the last days* foretold by Isaiah (Hebrews 1:1; 1 Peter 1:20). He said Jerusalem was guilty of shedding all the blood of all the righteous and all of that blood would be required on her *in his generation* (Matthew 23:29-39). I hope you will take the time to see what Jesus had to say about the vindication of the martyrs, and when it was to occur. Matthew 23 is critically important for the understanding of the Bible doctrine of the vindication of the martyrs. Jesus *invariably* promised vindication of that righteous blood *in his generation*.

A look now at how Jesus uses Isaiah 2-4 confirms our application of that prophecy to an in-history Day of the Lord in judgment on Israel. In Luke 23:28-31, Jesus was being led to his crucifixion. As he carried his cross, the women who loved him wept for him. He turned to them and said:

"Daughters of Jerusalem, weep not for me, but weep for yourselves, and for your children. For, behold, the days are coming, in the which they shall say, Blessed are the barren, and the wombs that never bare, and the paps which never gave suck. Then shall they begin to say to the mountains, Fall on us; and to the hills, Cover us."

Jesus is alluding directly to Isaiah 2:10, 19, 21, (parallel Hosea 10:8). The Lucan passage is widely acknowledged to apply to the impending judgment of Jerusalem. *This means that Jesus applied Isaiah's prophecy of the Day of the Lord, to the coming judgment of Judah in AD 70.* This is incredibly important.

Not only does Jesus apply Isaiah 2-4, and its prediction of the Day of Jehovah to his generation, *Paul does also*, in 2 Thessalonians 1:4-12. The apostle promised the suffering Christians that they would receive, "rest when the Lord

Jesus is revealed from heaven in flaming fire,[6] taking vengeance on them that know not God and that obey not the Gospel...these shall be punished with everlasting destruction from the presence of the Lord and from the glory of his power." Verse nine, as noted above, is an *exact quote* from the Septuagint of Isaiah 2:10, 19, 21.

Before progressing to what Paul said about this issue, it is important to remind you that in the Old Testament, Jehovah came in judgment of Israel and Jerusalem, *for shedding innocent blood*. Ezekiel said the destruction of Jerusalem at the hands of the Babylonians was the *Day of the Lord* (Ezekiel 7:19). It was not only the Day of the Lord's Wrath, it was coming on them because they had shed innocent blood (Ezekiel 9:9).

The *time and context* of that Day of the Lord was the *in history* judgment of Jerusalem in BC 586 at the hands of the Chaldean king, Nebuchadnezzar. The *language* of that Day of the Lord was clearly metaphoric. Jehovah did not visibly come and destroy earth and end time. That is pretty clear, isn't it? He came to *avenge the innocent blood* shed by Jerusalem (Ezekiel 9:9).

So, the Lord *came* in BC 586 in the judgment of Jerusalem, for shedding innocent blood. The language of his coming was patently metaphoric having nothing to do with a literal, end of time, visible coming of the Lord. We then find Messianic predictions of the last days that foretold the coming of the Lord to avenge the blood of the righteous. Jesus said that he was coming to fulfill those prophecies *in his generation, in the judgment of Judah.* What authority do we have for making that a prediction of a literal, end of time, visible coming of Christ out of heaven? We turn now to what Paul had to say about this Day of the Lord to avenge the blood of His saints.

Paul, living in the last days (1 Corinthians 10:11) promised the Thessalonians that their suffering would be vindicated, "when the Lord Jesus is revealed from heaven" to bring tribulation on their tormentors. Paul said their persecutors, "shall be punished with everlasting destruction from the presence of the Lord, and the glory of his power."

---

[6] 2 Thessalonians 1:8 is a citation of Isaiah 66:15 and the Lord's coming with fire to judge the wicked. The passage, like Isaiah 2-4, is a prediction of the judgment on Israel. Thus, Paul not only directly quotes from Isaiah 2-4, and its prediction of the last days fall of Jerusalem, he also cites from Isaiah's prediction of the fall of Jerusalem to bring in the New Heavens and Earth. This is sort of a "double whammy" that demands application of Thessalonians to AD 70.

Let's not forget that in his first epistle Paul said the same thing, when he spoke of how the Jews had killed the prophets, Jesus and were now persecuting the apostles and prophets of Jesus. He said that the judgment on Judah was even then overhanging them (1 Thessalonians 2:15-17.) In other words, 1 Thessalonians 2:15-17 says the same thing as 2 Thessalonians 1. Virtually *no one* denies that 1 Thessalonians 2 is a referent to the AD 70 judgment. Well, if 1 Thessalonians 2 is about the AD 70 coming of the Lord, then 2 Thessalonians 1 is about the AD 70 coming of the Lord, because *both texts discuss the identical issues*, persecution of the Thessalonians and they both promise imminent vindication and judgment.[7] This brings up a very important point.

In Isaiah the prophecy is about the last days judgment *of Israel*. In Luke 23 Jesus applies Isaiah to the impending judgment of *Jerusalem*. Now, in 2 Thessalonians 1, Paul is quoting Isaiah to predict the imminent judgment on the persecutors of the church: "it is a righteous thing with God to repay them that are troubling you" (2 Thessalonians 1:6). That is, without any doubt a reference to the Jews. Read Acts 17 and 1 Thessalonians 2:15f again. Now, if the Jews were the persecutors and if Christ was going to judge their persecutors at his revelation this demands that *Paul was predicting the judgment of Israel at his coming.*

So, if we apply 2 Thessalonians 1 to the future we must take the position that Paul is predicting that the Jews will one day, once again, persecute the church. So much so, that they will be the focus of Christ's coming to judge them. Do you believe that? I surely don't, and frankly, *I don't know of anyone* that does. It is not Biblical. Yet, if we are going to apply 2 Thessalonians 1 to the future we have to take that position.

The only way to avoid this position is to say that the identity of the persecutors is irrelevant. It was not the *Thessalonians* being persecuted and that Paul was focused on persecutors and persecuted in a distant time and place. That violates the specific wording of the text, however.

But to repeat, the point that must not be missed is that 2 Thessalonians 1:9 *is a direct quote from the prophecy in Isaiah that Jesus applied to his coming against Jerusalem in his generation.* It is obvious that Jesus (Luke 23) did not apply Isaiah's prediction to an end of time Day of the Lord. Jesus and Paul quote from the identical verses in Isaiah.

---

[7] I have presented the material in this book in public debate on several occasions, noting the absolute parallelism between 1 Thessalonians 2:15f and 2 Thessalonians 1. I have not, to this day, had a single response to the argument.

Jesus applied Isaiah to AD 70 (Luke 23:28f). Paul quotes from the same verses that Jesus applied to AD 70. So, if Jesus applied those verses to the AD 70 judgment of Israel, what is our evidence that Paul was changing the application? Paul gives *no indication* that he is applying Isaiah differently from Jesus. As a matter of fact, the motif of vindication of the martyrs is identical. This is important.

There is another connection between Isaiah 2-4 and 2 Thessalonians 1. Isaiah said that in the last days, the "Branch of the Lord," that is Jesus, would come to be *glorified* (4:1-2). This would be the time when He came in judgment of Jerusalem for shedding innocent blood (4:4). In 2 Thessalonians Paul quotes from Isaiah 2. He predicts the judgment of the Jews for persecuting the saints and says that this would occur when Christ came to be "glorified in his saints." See the connection? These parallels prove that Paul did have Isaiah's prophecy in mind and shows positively that he did not have an end of time, visible coming of Christ in mind. He was predicting the judgment of Old Covenant Judah.

Here is what we have in 2 Thessalonians 1. Paul promised vindication of the suffering saints and vengeance against the persecutors at the coming of the Lord. The source for his promise is Isaiah 2-4, the promise that in the last days, in the *Day of the Lord, Jehovah* would judge *Israel* for shedding the blood of the righteous (Isaiah 4:2f).

Isaiah's prediction is patently not an *end of time* prophecy but a prediction of a historical Day of the Lord against Old Covenant Jerusalem.

Jesus cites *the identical verses that Paul quotes* to predict the fall of Jerusalem for shedding his blood (Luke 23).

Thus, Isaiah 2-4 predicted a historical Day of the Lord. Jesus applied Isaiah 2-4 to a historical Day of the Lord. Paul quotes *the same verses* from Isaiah that Jesus does, and promises the same thing, vindication/vengeance, as Isaiah and Jesus did. It is inconceivable that Paul would be applying Isaiah to a Day of the Lord totally different in nature and far removed in time, than where Isaiah and Jesus placed it. Paul was *not* radically transforming Isaiah's prediction. Rather, he too was anticipating the Day of the Lord against Israel, for persecuting the saints and that occurred with the fall of Jerusalem in AD 70.

The failure to acknowledge the Old Testament source of 2 Thessalonians 1 is a major, fatal flaw in the interpretative view of the amillennial and postmillennial worlds especially. Paul in Thessalonians was, like Jesus, anticipating the fulfillment of God's Old Covenant promises to Israel. Those promises included the judgment of Judah for shedding the blood of the martyrs.

11

The interpretation of 2 Thessalonians hinges then on Jesus' interpretation of Isaiah 2-4. Paul says that at the *parousia*[8] which he describes in typical Old Testament language of the Day of Jehovah, the persecutors would be persecuted and they would be cast out of the presence of the Lord (2 Thessalonians 1:9-10).

Two more questions help our understanding of Thessalonians.

First, who was it that the New Testament constantly refers to as the persecutor of the church and as a result of that persecution was to be rejected? Without doubt Paul was speaking of: "Those who are troubling you." And that means that it was none other than Old Covenant Judah (Matthew 21; Acts 7:52f; Galatians 4:22f, 1 Thessalonians 2:15-17, etc.). Let me drive this home.

So, again, Paul said Christ would repay with tribulation, "those who are troubling you."

☞ A Man of Sin, from the Eastern European Common Market was not the one troubling, i.e. persecuting, the Thessalonians.

☞ A Man of Sin and his minions, based in literal Babylon of Iraq was not, "those who are troubling you."

☞ The Roman Catholic pope was not the entity guilty of being, "those who are troubling you."

☞ The Roman empire was not, "those who are troubling you."[9]

☞ "Those who are troubling you" if we are going to deal exegetically with the text, the context and the facts of history, *were none other than the Jews.*

---

[8] *Parousia* is a Greek word meaning *presence*, not *coming*. In the OT, when Jehovah acted He was "present," but not visibly. His "presence" was manifested, symbolized, by His sovereign use of nature or nations to accomplish His purposes.

[9] The popular view that the Romans were the chief persecutors of the church in the first century is false, as an increasing number of scholars and Bible students are coming to realize.. Robert Briggs, *Jewish Temple Imagery in the Book of Revelation*, Studies in Biblical Literature, Vol. 10, (New York, Peter Lang Publishing, 1999)37 says, "There is no good evidence that any Emperor before Decius (mid-third century) issued a general edict against Christianity." He continues, "The alleged evidence for a Domitianic persecution against Christians turns out on closer scrutiny to be highly nebulous at best and therefore ought to be dismissed as illusory." See my *Who Is This Babylon* for a fuller discussion of this issue.

While it may true that the Jews stirred others up against the church in Thessalonica (Acts 17) at least briefly, the indisputable fact is that it was the Jews who were the movers and shakers of the persecution. They, and they alone, must be identified as "those who are troubling you."

Second, who was it that had dwelt in the presence of God, but was now being threatened with expulsion from that favored place? Answer: It was Old Covenant Judah. This is critical, yet mostly ignored, so let me reiterate: Only one people ever dwelt in the presence of the Lord but would be cast out of that presence for persecuting the saints.

As proof of this, consider Galatians 4:22f. Paul discusses Old Covenant Jerusalem "the Jerusalem that now is" as he puts it, and the New Jerusalem. He speaks of two covenants, two seeds. The seed after the "flesh" was the Old Covenant nation. The "old seed" was dwelling in the house with the children of promise. The problem was that the Old Covenant people were now persecuting the "children of the promise" i.e. *the children of Abraham by faith.* As a result of persecuting the Christians, the children of the flesh *were now to be cast out of the house of God.* This is the picture of 2 Thessalonians 1. Those who dwelt in the presence of God were to be cast out for persecuting the seed of promise.

Another thought on this. If 2 Thessalonians, like Galatians 4, speaks of the casting out of the nation of Judah from the presence of the Lord, then that means that if 2 Thessalonians 1 has not been fulfilled, *the Jews remain in the presence of God*, in covenant relationship with Him. The kingdom has not been taken from them (Matthew 21:43). This means nothing less than that the Old Covenant remains in effect as well.[10] Do you see the serious nature of denying the fulfillment of the text?

Isaiah 2-4, the passage Paul quotes in 2 Thessalonians, proves that it was *the Old Covenant people* that was to be cast out of the presence of the Lord, for persecuting the saints. This language of being in the presence of the Lord, before His face, is the language of *covenant*. In other words, when Israel was obedient she stood before God's face. *She dwelt in His presence.* Check out Numbers 6:25; Psalms 16:11; Psalms 100:2, etc.

On the other hand, anytime Israel or Judah sinned, Jehovah threatened to *cast them out of His presence*, or to hide His face from them: Deuteronomy 31:17, Deuteronomy 32:20 (This latter text speaks of Israel's last days, the time in

---

[10] See the Preston - Simmons Debate book: *The End of Torah, At the Cross or AD 70*, for a demonstration that the Law of Moses passed away in AD 70. The debate book is available from my websites.

which Paul wrote. He even applies this prophetic chapter to his generation and personal ministry) Ezekiel 7:22; 14:8; 15:7; 39:23-29; Jeremiah 4:26; 5:22; see especially Jeremiah 23:39, 52:3 also.

There is something very important to note. It is *never* said, *anywhere* in the Old Testament, that a pagan nation or people was *cast out of the presence of the Lord*. What is said is that the Lord *came*, in some instances, against pagan nations and in those instances they were destroyed "at His presence" (See Isaiah 19:1; Nahum 1:5). There is a huge difference between being cast out from His presence and being destroyed, "at His presence." Those, "cast out of the presence of the Lord" were His people being punished for their sin. Those punished "at His presence" were His enemies being punished, in most cases, for their actions *against His people*.

In 2013, I debated popular talk show host Steve Gregg, in Denver, Colorado. I made the argument above concerning being cast out of the presence of the Lord demanding a previous covenantal relationship. The force of the argument was telling on Gregg– who was a gracious opponent– and he finally argued that it was not the persecutors that were to be cast out of the presence of the Lord, but, that the punishment on the persecutors was coming from the presence of the Lord.[11] But, this does help, since the context still identifies the persecutors as the Jews!

Take another look at Isaiah 2-4, the source of Paul's prediction in 2 Thessalonians 1. Isaiah foretold the last days and Paul was living in the last days, as we have seen. Isaiah foretold the judgment of *Israel* (3:13f). Paul is concerned with the judgment of those persecuting the church, i.e. the Jews (1 Thessalonians 2:15-17). Isaiah foretold the judgment of *Israel* for shedding innocent blood (4:4) just as Paul does. Isaiah said that *Israel* would flee, "from the terror of the Lord, and the glory of his majesty" (2:10, 19, 21) and Paul, *quoting these verses*, says that the persecutors - Israel - would be cast out of the presence of the Lord.

Our point is that Isaiah's prophecy of the last days was concerned, not with pagan nations or America, or Russia, or who ever. It was a prophecy of what *was to happen to Israel in her last days*. She was to be cast out of the presence of the Lord and judged for shedding innocent blood. Since Paul is using Isaiah as the source of his prediction, this means that Paul was not predicting the "end of time" or the end of the Christian Age. He was not speaking of some unknown, far distant persecutor of the church in some future generation. He was predicting

---

[11] DVDs of that debate are available from my websites: www.eschatology.org, or www.bibleprophecy.com.

the end of the Old Covenant Age of Israel; that occurred with the destruction of Jerusalem and the Temple in AD 70.

A quick word here. Paul's statement that Israel was to be cast out of the presence of the Lord is to be understood *corporately*, to speak of the *nation*. Paul was not saying that Jews, individually, would never be able to accept the Messiah. Israel was the chosen people for centuries, but was a mere shadow of "better things to come," and those better things are Christ and his body. When Christ and his New Covenant world was fully in place, the shadow world of the Old Covenant was supposed to pass away, i.e. be "cast out of His presence." So, *Paul is not speaking of the damnation of individuals in hell.* He was saying that when Christ came in judgment of Judah for persecuting the saints, *that Old Covenant nation would be cast out, forever.* This clearly precludes the events of 1948 from being the fulfillment of prophecy.[12] It likewise falsifies any attempt to make Paul out to be predicting a yet future conversion and salvation of "all Israel" at the Second Coming of Christ (Romans 11:25f). If what we are saying is correct, it patently denies a future restoration of Israel.[13]

Jesus said his disciples would be persecuted, but that their persecutors, the Jews, would have the tables turned against them in judgment (Matthew 23-24). This is *precisely* the pattern of 2 Thessalonians. Further, there is no reason for delineating between the promised wrath against the persecutors in 1 Thessalonians 2:15f, and the promise against the persecutors in 2 Thessalonians

---

[12] See my book *Israel 1948: Countdown to No Where*, for proof that 1948 had nothing to do with the fulfillment of prophecy. Available from our website: www.eschatology.org.

[13] In June of 2014, I had a formal Internet debate with prominent Zionist apologist Dr. Michael Brown. The focus of our attention was Romans 11:25f. Dr. Brown affirms a yet future salvation of a significant majority of "Israel" at the parousia of Christ. I argued that when one examines the prophetic background and source of Romans 11:25f– Isaiah 27 / 59– that it precludes a future application. Both Isaiah 27 and 59 foretold the salvation of Israel (the remnant) at the time when Israel would be judged for shedding innocent blood. Jesus unambiguously posited that at the AD 70 judgment and destruction of Jerusalem. These arguments had an undeniable impact on Dr. Brown. That debate is archived on YouTube: https://www.youtube.com/watch?v=H1fP1xB1gsM. At the time I am writing this, that debate has been viewed almost 21,000 times.

1. The chain of progression is direct, Matthew 23 ☛ 1 Thessalonians 2:15-17 ☛ 2 Thessalonians 1. Matthew 23 controls Thessalonians and the discussion of the vindication of the martyrs at *the Day of the Lord Jesus Christ.* That judgment was coming against *Israel.*

If being punished "with everlasting destruction from the presence of the Lord" for persecuting the followers of Christ referred to the punishment of Judah / Israel - as Galatians 4 confirms– this means there cannot be a yet future conversion and salvation of "all Israel."

It means that Old Covenant Israel was cast out of the presence of the Lord – *forever* – when Jerusalem was judged and destroyed for persecuting the New Covenant Seed of Messiah.

TRIBULATION AND RELIEF
THLIPSIS AND *ANESIS*

We are going to do a bit of a Greek word study, but I don't want that to scare you, because it is very important. It is also pretty simple. I think you will find it helpful. In 2 Thessalonians 1:4-12, the apostle calls attention, *four times*, to the present suffering being endured by the Thessalonians. (Remember that the Jews had instigated that persecution, Acts 17.) He uses the Greek word *thlipsis*, translated tribulation, to speak of that persecution. This is the word used by Jesus to foretell what was to happen to his disciples prior to the fall of Jerusalem and is exactly what was happening in Thessalonians (Matthew 24:9).

Thlipsis is used some 45 times in the NT and in all but a few texts refers to *persecution for the cause of Christ*. The word originally meant pressure and could refer to any kind of pressure, even financial pressure (2 Corinthians 8:13). On the other hand, the antonym of *thlipsis* is *anesis*. This word, when used with *thlipsis*, invariably means *relief* from whatever kind of pressure is being endured. So, *thlipsis* is pressure, in Thessalonians the pressure of persecution. *Anesis* is relief from pressure. In Thessalonians, it is therefore, *relief from persecution.* That was easy, right? Easy and *important*.

Now, I am going to say something that is so *simple* that you might be tempted to wonder why I am saying it, but, it is important, and so ignored, that I have to point it out. Remember the old saying that sometimes we can't see the forest for the trees? Well, that is what happens most of the time when we read Thessalonians. We read it and overlook the most obvious facts of the text. And what is it that is so *obvious*, but so *overlooked*? It is the fact that for Jesus to give the Thessalonians relief from their persecution, at his coming, that the Thessalonians, get that, the *Thessalonians*, had to be under the pressure of persecution *at the time of Jesus' coming*. Jesus could not give the Thessalonians relief "when the Lord Jesus is revealed from heaven," if the *Thessalonians* were not, or will not be under the pressure of persecution at his coming.

The suffering of the Thessalonians and the time of the Lord's coming are same time events. So, if the first century Thessalonians are all dead and we are on safe ground to say they are, then either Christ came in their lifetime and gave them relief, or he failed to come and give them relief. It is that simple. The problem is that inescapable.

17

> **How could Jesus give the Thessalonians relief from persecution at his coming, if his coming is yet future and the Thessalonians are all dead? The fact is that the Thessalonians had to be, or have to be, under the pressure of *persecution*, at the time of the Lord's coming, or he could not give them relief from persecution "when the Lord is revealed."**

I can hardly over emphasize the importance of the *thlipsis* versus *anesis* contrast. As just noted, the word *thlipsis* means pressure; *anesis* is relief from pressure.[14] (I am unaware of any instance of *anesis* meaning *reward*).When *anesis* and *thlipsis* appear together, *anesis* is *invariably* relief from whatever pressure is being endured. Paul speaks of the tribulation being endured by the Thessalonians. This affliction was a "manifest token" of the tribulation (*thlipsis*) coming upon the persecutors (v. 4-5). Paul promised that the Thessalonians would be given "rest (*anesis*) with us when the Lord Jesus is revealed from heaven." What virtually all commentators do is to turn Paul's prediction into a promise that at the coming of the Lord, Christians will be delivered from the stress and strain of the human experience.[15] There will be no more cancer, no more heart attacks, no more financial pressure, etc.. I recently heard popular evangelist Adrian Rogers make this application. However, *this is not what Paul was talking about.* Paul was promising *relief from persecution.*

Significantly, the persecutors of the Thessalonians would receive "in kind" what they were giving the Thessalonians (v. 6). They were "pressuring" the Thessalonians. However, at the *parousia*, Jesus would give "pressure" (*thlipsis*) to them. Now, unless the Jewish persecutors of the saints were sending the

---

[14] *Exegetical Dictionary of the New Testament*, Balz-Schneider, Vol. 1, (Grand Rapids, Eerdmans, 1990)97.

[15] I have heard countless ministers utilize 2 Thessalonians 1 in this manner. It seems, at least in my experience, that ministers give no consideration whatsoever to the real life situation of the *Thessalonians* and Paul's promise to *them*. John MacArthur appeals to this text as proof that Christians see the promise of Christ's return "as a great comfort for the people of God in their times of trial." John MacArthur, *The Second Coming*, (Wheaton, Ill. Crossways Publishing, 1999)48. For MacArthur, the trials are not necessarily persecution, but the human existence.

Christians to hell (i.e. *thlipsis*) then since the persecutors were going to receive what they were giving, one cannot twist Thessalonians to mean that Christ was going to send them to hell, in the way the passage is normally understood. *The persecutors were going to receive what they were giving.* This is, of course, exactly what Jesus foretold in Matthew 23:33-36, as well as in Matthew 24:9-21. The tables would be turned, *the persecutors would become the persecuted.* Needless to say, this is precisely what happened in the Jewish/Roman War.

The *consistent* New Testament testimony is that the first-century saints, being persecuted for Christ, were about to receive vindication and relief from their persecution at the parousia (Romans 8:18; 2 Corinthians 4:16f; Hebrews 10:26-37; 1 Peter 1:5-7; Revelation). Either this promise was the expression of a hope ultimately disappointed, or it was fulfilled.

Thessalonians was written as an "occasional letter," that is, a specific historical occasion prompted Paul to write. He wrote to address a very specific, very real problem in the lives of living breathing humans in approximately AD 50-52. Unfortunately many good folks completely ignore the "occasional" nature of the book and make it apply to people and events totally unrelated to the lives of the first century Christians being persecuted for their faith. What happens to "audience relevance" when this is done, however? Wasn't the epistle written to *them*, about *their* problem, offering a solution to *them*? Indeed. What right then do we have to distort the text into a prediction of events unrelated to them, about events that would offer them no comfort, at a time far removed from them?

Thessalonians was written to the *Thessalonians* who were being persecuted in their own city, 2000 years ago. They, (nor Paul) were not thinking of a yet future persecution against Christians in New York City. Their persecution was on their own streets. And, Paul, *by inspiration*, promised relief from that persecution at the parousia

Perhaps we should ask this question: *Is God in the business of giving false hope?* There is no doubt, when one reads Thessalonians with an unbiased mind, that Paul was writing to living people, experiencing real persecution. There is no doubt that Paul was writing to give them hope amid the pain and that hope was that God would give them "rest, with us, when the Lord Jesus is revealed from heaven." *Paul was promising real people real relief from real persecution.*

Unfortunately, the common interpretation of the text says that Paul was not speaking to the Thessalonians about their time and their suffering, not *really*. Paul was talking about the church at least 2000 years away, promising *them* that *they* would receive relief at the *parousia*. One can only marvel at how such a promise could be a genuine comfort to the Thessalonians. They were suffering and dying, yet Paul told them that *one day*, Jesus would give the last generation of Christians relief from *their* suffering. Wouldn't the Thessalonians have the right to ask: "Okay, Paul, what about *us*, though? What about *our present persecution*? Is Jesus going to give *us* relief?" Tragically, most commentators tell us that Paul would have said: "No, I am really sorry guys, but I can't offer *you* any promise of relief from *your* persecution. I can only tell you that the last generation of Christians will receive relief from *their* persecution."

The writer of Proverbs said, "Hope deferred makes the heart sick" (Proverbs 13:12). Paul did in fact give the Thessalonians the hope, more, the *assurance*, that Jesus was *coming in their lifetime* to give *them* relief from persecution. *Did God disappoint them*? If Paul gave the Thessalonians a false hope, a hope not fulfilled by the coming of Jesus, then Paul was a false prophet, the inspiration of scripture fails. Jesus is not the Son of God. The issue is that serious.

It is very common to hear folks say, "The Bible says what it means, and means what it says. Paul says Christ was coming, and I have not seen him, so he must not have come." The problem here is the failure to see that Christ was not supposed to come bodily and visibly. He was supposed to come through the judgment of Old Covenant Judah. He *did* do that when Jerusalem fell in AD 70.

God "came" in the Old Testament and did so through the instrumentality of an invading army under His sovereign control. No one saw Jehovah come on the clouds against Egypt, but He came (Isaiah 19-20). He came against Judah, BC 586, by means of the Babylonian army and cast Judah out of His presence (Jeremiah 23:39) but they did not see Him coming. Not visibly.

Likewise Jesus said he was going to come "in the glory of the Father" (Matthew 16:27) and in judgment in the same way he had seen the Father judge (John 5:19-23).[16] Since we know that this is what Isaiah 2-4 predicted and since we know that Jesus applied Isaiah to the judgment of Israel, then, this demands that this is what Paul was predicting in 2 Thessalonians 1. He was not talking about a visible, bodily coming of Christ out of heaven on a cumulus cloud.

Did God lie to the Thessalonians when He, through Paul, promised to give them relief from their real life persecution? If God wanted to promise the

---

[16] See my book, *Like Father Like Son, On Clouds of Glory*, for a comprehensive study of this prediction. The belief in a physical, bodily coming of Christ is the cause of a belief that he has failed to keep his promises, since he said he was coming in the first century. The book is available from our website: www.eschatology.or, or www.bibleprophecy.com. It is also available from Amazon and Kindle.

20

Thessalonians that they were going to receive relief from that persecution at the coming of the Lord, how much clearer could He have communicated that truth? Imagine this scene with me.

You live in Thessalonica and you and your family have just made the decision to join the band of believers calling themselves Christians. You have heard Paul preach from the Law and the Prophets about Jesus and he has convinced you that Jesus really is the Messiah long hoped for. You have joined the community of believers through baptism, knowing well that this public action would bring public ridicule and ostracism.

In the days and months after accepting Jesus, the animosity of the community grows more intense. Paul has himself been run out of town for fear of his life. Jewish instigators are stirring up the community against your new found faith and fellowship. The ostracism grows more intense, even violent. Some members of the new faith community have now died publicly at the hands of the mobs.

Every Sunday, you meet, secretly with your new brothers and sisters to encourage and be encouraged. Then, a letter from Paul arrives. It is his second one and he has something to say about the persecution. Paul expresses his appreciation for the faith of the new community. He is fully aware of the suffering being endured. But, he says: "it is a righteous thing with God to repay with tribulation those who trouble you, and to give you who are troubled rest with us when the Lord Jesus is revealed from heaven with His mighty angels."

Let me ask you, if you knew that Christ would "come" as his Father had come in the OT, (i.e. non-literally, but through the instrumentality of other nations) if you heard Paul's words read in the assembly, under the circumstances described above, would you get the idea that the promised relief was thousands of years away? Would you get the idea that your persecutors would continue to persecute you for the rest of your life? Put yourself in that assembly 2000 years ago, hearing those words of promise. What would be the relevance for the Thessalonians if Paul was not talking about their world, their suffering and was not promising them any hope of relief?

People today complain that applying Paul's promises to the Thessalonians to whom he was writing makes the Bible irrelevant for us today. Well, if honoring the fact that the book was written to people 2000 years ago makes it irrelevant to us, what does it do to take a book written directly to them, and saying it actually had nothing to do with them? Does that not make the Thessalonian epistles irrelevant to the very people to whom it was written?

Kenneth Gentry, writing about the book of Revelation and why it cannot be interpreted as a prediction of a yet future coming of the Lord, makes the following comment:

"Another detriment to the strained interpretations listed above is that John was writing to historical churches existing in his own day (Rev. 1:4). He and they are presently suffering "tribulation' (Rev. 1:9a). John's message (ultimately from Christ 1:1) calls upon each to give careful, spiritual attention to his words (2:7 etc). John is deeply concerned with the expectant cry of the martyrs and the divine promise of their soon vindication (6:10; cp. 5:3-5). He (John, dkp) would be cruelly mocking their circumstances (while committing a 'verbal scam' according to Mounce)."[17]

Now let me ask you this: how much different is Thessalonians from the situation in Revelation? Were the Thessalonians suffering real persecution just like the churches of Asia? Yes. Were the churches in Asia any more "historical churches" than the church at Thessalonica? Hardly. Did Paul expect the Thessalonians to pay any less attention to his words than John demanded in Revelation? Of course not. Was John's promise of relief from persecution any more real and urgent than Paul's promise to the Thessalonians? *Absolutely not.*

The fact is that *the situations in Thessalonica and Asia were identical.* And the apostles promised their audiences the same thing, relief from persecution at Christ's coming. Interestingly, Gentry says that if John was not promising the Asian churches real relief from their persecution *for their lifetime*, that Revelation loses all audience relevance and John would have been committing a "verbal scam" on those suffering Christians.

Well, *I agree with Gentry.* I think he presents a convincing and compelling case. My question is, why do the excellent principles that he applies to Revelation not apply to Thessalonians? *Why won't Mr. Gentry, and others like him, be consistent in the application of these solid interpretive principles?* You see, Mr. Gentry, in spite of his excellent hermeneutic in Revelation, applies 2 Thessalonians 1 to a yet future coming of the Lord at the end of time.[18]

---

[17] Kenneth Gentry, *The Beast of Revelation*, Revised, (Powder Springs, GA, American Vision, 2002)27. Available from my websites.

[18] Kenneth Gentry, *He Shall Have Dominion*, (Institute For Christian Economics, Tyler, Tx., 1992)386.

To do this, Gentry must claim that while Paul *seems* to have been writing to living humans in the midst of real persecution, and while it *sounds* like he was offering *them* relief from that very real tribulation, that in reality, he was not speaking to *them*, or about *them*. He was not promising *them* anything and most assuredly he was not promising that Christ would give *them* relief at his coming.[19] Such an argument is clearly a mark of total desperation to avoid the undeniable statements of the text. *Every rule of proper hermeneutics has to be perverted, mitigated, or ignored, to deny that Paul was addressing the Thessalonians about their real life problem and promising them relief from that persecution, at the parousia.*

To apply 2 Thessalonians to the future, we have to deny or ignore that it was written "to the church of the Thessalonians" (2 Thessalonians 1:1) or ignore or deny that it was written about their present problem and make Paul's words apply to people not even alive, not suffering at the time. We have to ignore the historical fact of who was persecuting them as well.

This means that the Thessalonians had the perfect right to ask why Paul would even bother to write *them* such a letter. It had nothing to do with *them* and promised *them* nothing. Why would Paul even bother to write to the suffering Thessalonians to tell them that one day, by and by, perhaps two millennia or more removed, that some Christians would be suffering for Christ and that at *that time* Christ would return and give *them* relief from their suffering? Again, wouldn't the Thessalonians have the right to ask, "But what about *us*, Paul? What about *our* suffering, right *now*?"

WHAT PAUL DID NOT SAY

Let me reiterate here what Paul *definitely did say*: **1.)** *He did say* that the Thessalonians were being persecuted at the time he wrote: "To you who are being troubled" (v. 7). This is undeniable. **2.)** *He did say* that they would receive relief from that persecution (v. 7). This is undeniable. **3.)** *He did say* that the promised relief from that persecution would be given, "when the Lord Jesus is revealed from heaven." This is *undeniable*.

Now, it is important to be reminded of what Paul did say, because in order to avoid the clear cut meaning of these statements it is often argued that Paul was

---

[19]   This was in fact the very argument that Thomas Thrasher made in my debate with him in Alabama. When I pressed my question: "Did Christ come and give the Thessalonians relief from their real life persecution?" Thrasher said Paul never promised the Thessalonians relief at the parousia.

23

not actually promising the *Thessalonians* that Christ was coming in their lifetime to give them relief. Again, this is an argument born of desperation, not of the text, but it is really the only recourse that the futurists have. Well, if Paul was not saying that Christ was coming in the lifetime of the Thessalonians, to give *them* relief from persecution, *what in the world was he saying?* What do words *mean*, anyway? And what *was* Paul offering *them*, if he was not offering "*relief*"?

If we are going to deal candidly with the text, and in order to help answer these questions, we need to see what Paul *did not say*. We need to realize that words have to be imported into the text, *in violation of the words that are there*, in order to maintain a futurist application of the text. So, what did Paul *not say*?

✗ Paul *did not say*, "I want you Thessalonians to know that you will possibly die at the hands of your persecutors and when you die, *this* will be your relief from persecution." In other words, Paul did not say that death would be their relief from their persecution. He said they would receive "rest, with us, when the Lord Jesus is revealed from heaven." It would be the *parousia* of Christ to bring their anticipated and promised relief, not their death.

✗ Paul *did not say*, *"You will not receive any relief from your persecution in your lifetime*. You may actually die under the persecution. However, I want you to know that when the Lord eventually comes, someday, *you will be rewarded in heaven* for your faithfulness." Let me reiterate that the word *anesis* means *relief*, not reward. Paul was promising relief from the pressure of persecution. Paul did not tell the Thessalonians, "You will *not* receive relief when the Lord comes," which is what he should have said if the traditional view is correct.

✗ Paul *did not say*, "You will die and go to Abraham's bosom to wait the coming of the Lord at which time you will go to heaven." Please catch the power of what I am about to say. Of necessity, the *Thessalonians* would have to be, *or will have to be*, under persecution, "when the Lord Jesus is revealed from heaven," in order for Jesus to give *them*, "relief when the Lord Jesus is revealed." *Jesus could not give the Thessalonians relief from persecution when he comes, if they are not under the pressure of persecution when he comes.*

So, if Paul was writing to living breathing humans, under the pressure of persecution, and if he promised them relief from that pressure, "when the Lord Jesus is revealed" then, *prima facia*, they, the *Thessalonians* would (or *will*) have to be under the pressure of persecution, "when the Lord Jesus is revealed."

You need to know something. Every single commentary in my library, and that is quite a few, agrees that Paul was promising the rest, "when the Lord Jesus is revealed from heaven." *Everyone of them. No one* denies that the rest (relief) and the coming of the Lord are *same time events* in the text. The problem is that when it comes to *applying* the text, every single one of these commentators divorce the passage from the lives and the world of the Thessalonians. They divorce the suffering from the Thessalonians and apply it to the church in the future. They divorce the Jewish persecutors from the Thessalonians and make the persecutors to be some nameless entity and change the persecution into "life's difficulties." They divorce Christ's coming from that time and apply Paul's promise to *the last generation of Christians.*

My point is this: if the coming of the Lord, the persecution and the relief from that persecution are all *same time events*–and they unequivocally are in the text-- then it is the worst sort of distortion of the text to divorce the coming of the Lord from *the first century generation of the Thessalonians.* After all, to reiterate, Paul was writing, "to the church of the Thessalonians" about *their* suffering, *their* relief, *their* persecutors.

Now since, by the very nature of the case, the Thessalonians would have to be, or will have to be, under the pressure of persecution, "when the Lord Jesus is revealed from heaven," then if Paul had in mind that they would actually die and go to Abraham's bosom, this means that *Abraham's bosom is a place of pressure from which the Thessalonians would long for relief.* But, if Abraham's bosom is the pressure that they were under and from which they wanted relief, then this means that at the coming of Christ, *Abraham is given persecution.* Remember, Paul said that those pressuring the Thessalonians, would be given tribulation at the time of Christ's coming. So, if Abraham's bosom is the pressure that the Thessalonians are now under, then Abraham will be *tribulated* at Christ's coming. Do you see what happens when we ignore or distort the clear words of the text? We wind up making *really bad arguments.*

Let me reiterate: the Thessalonians would have to be under the pressure of persecution, "when the Lord Jesus is revealed from heaven." Paul did not say death then hades, then Christ's coming. He said persecution, but relief from persecution, *"when the Lord is revealed."*

The suggestion that the Thessalonians might die and go to Abraham's bosom to wait actually demands that *their death would be their relief.* But again, *this is not what Paul promised.* He promised relief from the persecution they were experiencing *while they were alive.* They would be alive, under the pressure of

25

persecution, but would receive relief from that on going pressure "when the Lord Jesus is revealed."

To identify *the death of the Thessalonians*, as the source and time of their relief, redefines Christ's coming as *the death of the Thessalonians*. After all, it was the *parousia* that would give them relief. So, if they were to receive *relief by dying,* then this defines their death as, "the revelation of Jesus Christ with his mighty angels, in flaming fire." Is that what Paul was *really* saying? Was Paul saying that as each individual Thessalonian Christian died, that Christ was, "revealed from heaven, with his angels, in flaming fire taking vengeance on those that know not God"? Just exactly how would Christ come in vengeance against the Thessalonian persecutors as each individual Thessalonian Christian died?

Consider this also. If they were to get relief from their persecution by their death, *perhaps at the hands of their persecutors*, then this means that *their persecutors are the ones that gave them relief.* But Paul said that they would receive relief from their persecutors "when the Lord Jesus is revealed from heaven." *He did not say*, "You will receive relief from your persecutors, *when your persecutors kill you*, or you die of natural causes."

It is evident that Paul did not say anything closely resembling what the traditional view needed for him to say. It is also evident that what Paul did say completely negates any possible futurist application of 2 Thessalonians 1 to an earth burning, time ending event. Christ was coming in the lifetime of the Thessalonians to give them relief from the persecution being brought against them by their Jewish countrymen.

This raises the question again: *Did Jesus come, in the lifetime of the Thessalonians and give them relief from the persecution that was raging against them in their streets, 2000 years ago? Yes or No?*

Now of course, virtually all modern Bible students will say "No, Jesus did not come and give the Thessalonians relief." However, for emphasis, let's take a look *one more time* at what Paul did write to the Thessalonians:

✔ *He did say* that the *Thessalonians* were being persecuted at the time he wrote. He did say this, didn't he?

✔ *He did say* that *they* would receive relief from that persecution. He did say this, didn't he?

✔ *He did say* that the promised relief would be given, "when the Lord Jesus is revealed from heaven." *And yes, he did say this, didn't he?*

Since these things are irrefutably true, then to make 2 Thessalonians a prediction of a yet future coming we must deny the words of the inspired text. We must *deny* that the *Thessalonians* were under persecution. But, we don't want to do that, *do we?* We must *deny* that Paul promised *them* relief from that persecution. Will we *do that*? Or, we must deny that Paul promised *them* relief from that persecution "when the Lord Jesus is revealed." Will we *do that*? Patently, we cannot deny any of these things and claim to take the Bible seriously. The text is too clear.

Since the textual statements are undeniable then what is the case if Christ did not come as most people still believe? It means, as noted above, that Paul's prediction failed. His apostolic promise to the Thessalonians failed. Paul is a false prophet and we are to reject all of his epistles.

Furthermore, if Paul's promise/prophecy failed, then clearly the inspiration of the entire NT corpus fails, for Paul claimed to write by the same Spirit that inspired the rest of the authors who, like Paul, claimed that Christ's coming was near in the first century.

In order to maintain faith in the inspiration of scriptures and the Deity of Christ we must believe that Christ came in the lifetime of the Thessalonians and gave them relief from their persecution. Now, as a matter of historical fact, the war of Rome in AD 66-70 did crush the organized and Roman sanctioned Jewish persecution of the church. This is an undeniable fact of history.

So, if we are willing to change our traditional concepts of "the revelation of Jesus Christ, with his mighty angels, in flaming fire," to conform to the Old Testament definition of the Day of the Lord then we can affirm that Paul was a true prophet. Jesus did come, in flaming fire and cast out the persecuting power, Old Covenant Judah, from His presence. God was faithful, inspiration is vindicated, faith confirmed, relief given.

2 THESSALONIANS AND REVELATION

Let me see if I can nail this down a bit more as we bring our study to a close. Remember that in 2 Thessalonians Paul was promising relief from persecution to those first century saints. He accused Old Covenant Jerusalem of persecuting the prophets of old, of killing Jesus and of persecuting the apostles and prophets of Jesus (1 Thessalonians 2:15f). He says the judgment on Israel for shedding the blood of the martyrs was near, very near. And in his prediction of the Lord's coming in judgment of the persecutors, Paul quotes directly from Isaiah 2-4.

What does this have to do with Revelation, you ask? *Virtually everything.* We will only be able to discuss this issue briefly here. In my *Who Is This Babylon* book, I discuss the issue in-depth.

1. As we have seen above, Paul was addressing the Thessalonians about their then present and on-going persecution. Likewise, John said he was the brother of his audience in tribulation, i.e. persecution. It was happening right then and there!

2. Not only was the persecution on-going when Paul and John wrote, that persecution was at the hands of the Jews. As we have shown in Thessalonians, "Those who are troubling you" is not a referent to Roman persecution, since the Romans did not begin persecuting the church until the time of Nero, well after the time when Paul wrote. In Revelation, while the Neronian persecution has begun, we cannot lose sight of the fact that even that "Roman persecution" was instigated and motivated by the Jews. I document this fully in my Babylon book.

3. In Revelation we have the martyrs who have been slain, praying for vindication and judgment on their persecutors (Revelation 6:9-11). Do you suppose that these martyrs– extending back to creation! - might be some of the prophets slain by Old Covenant Israel, the martyrs Jesus said would be vindicated at his coming against Jerusalem (Matthew 23)? We know this is true because the persecutor in Revelation had killed the prophets (16:6f). Do you see how this fits 1 Thessalonians 2:15 also, where Paul says that it was Old Covenant Israel that had killed *the prophets*?

4. The martyrs were told to "rest for a little while, until the number of their fellow servants and brethren, who should be killed as they were, was completed" (Revelation 6:11). Do you suppose that the saints who had to suffer before the judgment might include more of the *Thessalonians*, who had been suffering for

28

a good long while, and clearly, just like those under the altar, were crying out for relief[20] and judgment on their persecutors? Do you suppose that the filling up of the measure of the martyrs in Revelation is related to the filling up of the measure of sin in 1 Thessalonians 2:14f– the filling up of the measure of sin by persecuting the saints? Do you suppose it is related to Jesus' prediction that the number of the martyrs was to be filled in his generation (Matthew 23:29f) as he sent his apostles and prophets to Israel?

5. In Thessalonians, the persecutors were about to be judged at the coming of Christ in fulfillment of Isaiah's prophecy. In Revelation the prayer of the martyrs would be fulfilled in "a little while"(Revelation 6:9f). (Need we say that 2000 years *is not a little while*) in *the great day of the wrath of the lamb.*

What is so significant about John's promise is that in describing that coming day of judgment on the persecutors *he quotes directly from Isaiah 2*, *the identical verses* that Jesus in Luke 23 applied to the coming judgment of Jerusalem and *the identical verses* that Paul, in Thessalonians quoted in regard to the impending judgment of the persecutors of the Thessalonians. We know that the persecutions of the Thessalonians were instigated by the Jews. So, Isaiah 2-4 is about the last days judgment of *Israel* for shedding innocent blood. That is the way that Jesus and Paul applied it as well. Perfect consistency. But is that the way John was applying Isaiah, in Revelation? Yes indeed.

Notice that the martyrs cried out for judgment of their persecutor (Revelation 6:9f). The judgment coming on their persecutors was the Day of the Lord, in fulfillment of Isaiah 2-4. And who was the persecutor of the martyrs in Revelation? Well, real quickly, let's take note of a few facts.

The persecutor was *Babylon*, the mother of Harlots. And here is what she had done. *She had killed the prophets* (Revelation 16:6f). This refers to OT prophets. Only Old Covenant Jerusalem was guilty of that. See Luke 13:31f. *She had killed Jesus* (Revelation 11:8). Is there any doubt about where Jesus was slain? *She was*

---

[20] There is a difference between vindication and relief, although relief might come at the time of the vindication. Temporally, vindication and relief might be synchronous, but, they are nonetheless separate ideas. The saints in Revelation 6 did not need *relief*, however. They were clearly in a state of *rest*. (Different word than in 2 Thessalonians.) What they wanted was *vindication* and that was tied to the judgment of their persecutors on the earth. On the other hand, the Thessalonians, still living, wanted the *relief* that would come in the judgment of their tormentors.

killing the apostles and prophets of Jesus (Revelation 18:20, 24). Is there any question about who the Bible says killed the apostles and prophets of Jesus? If you have any doubts, see Matthew 23:34; Luke 11:49; 1 Thessalonians 2:15f.

The *only city* guilty of all those things was Old Covenant Jerusalem. Do you see how perfectly that fits Isaiah, Matthew 23, 1 and 2 Thessalonians? This is a perfect, consistent picture and it has nothing to do with a coming of the Lord at the end of time.

So, here is what we have.

Isaiah predicted the day of the Lord on Israel for shedding innocent blood. There is no way to construe his prediction to refer to a bodily, visible coming of the Lord.

Jesus applies Isaiah to the coming judgment on Jerusalem for killing him (Luke 23).

Paul quotes from the identical verses that Jesus applied to AD 70, to predict the coming judgment of the persecutors of the saints.

John quotes from *the identical verses of Isaiah used by Jesus and Paul*, to predict the soon coming judgment of "Babylon," the city, "where the Lord was slain" and guilty of killing the saints.

So: Isaiah, Jesus, Paul and John all addressed the same problem. The guilt of shedding innocent blood.

Isaiah, Jesus, Paul and John all wrote about the same time, the last days.

Isaiah, Jesus, Paul and John all made the same promise, the coming of the Lord to avenge the blood of the martyrs.

We know that Isaiah was not speaking of a bodily, visible, end of time coming of the Lord. We know that is not what Jesus was predicting when he cited Isaiah and we know that John was predicting Jesus' coming in the judgment of Jerusalem as well.

So, Paul is citing the *identical prophecy* that Jesus and John applied to the judgment of Israel in AD 70

Paul is addressing *the same problem* as Jesus and John, i.e. the vindication of the martyrs and judgment of the persecutors.

So, just how and why are we to think that Paul is applying Isaiah totally differently from Jesus and John? Should we not have some contextual indicator, some delineation, some statement from Paul that he is making a radically different application? The consistent use of Isaiah demands that we understand that Paul was predicting the AD 70 coming of the Lord to judge Israel for shedding the blood of the saints.

2 THESSALONIANS 1 AND THE RAPTURE

We can't close this work without an important observation on 2 Thessalonians 1 and its impact on the dispensational rapture doctrine. Virtually all dispensationalists apply 2 Thessalonians 1:7f to the Second Coming.[21] But here is the problem.

If 2 Thessalonians 1 is a prediction of the Second Coming it refutes everything the millennialists believe about the rapture and the tribulation, and here is why.

According to millennialists, the church will not be on earth, *at all*, during the Great Tribulation, i.e. at the time of the Second Coming of the Lord. Dwight Pentecost is emphatic, "The silence in the epistles (concerning the church and the Great Tribulation, DKP) which would leave the church unprepared for the tribulation argues for her complete absence from that period altogether."[22] According to the millennialists the church is removed from earth at the rapture.

2 Thessalonians 1 was written *to the church* at Thessalonica. (1:2) undergoing persecution (tribulation) and promised that the *church (not Israel)* would be given relief from that tribulation *at the Second Coming*. The importance of this cannot be stressed enough.

If the church is not on earth at the Second Coming, *how could Paul promise the church relief from tribulation at the Second Coming?* It does not matter if you are talking about simple tribulation or the Great Tribulation. If the church is not on earth she cannot experience either one. But 2 Thessalonians 1 depicts the church as undergoing tribulation at the time of the Second Coming. It would be Christ's Second Coming that would give, "relief when the Lord Jesus is revealed from heaven."

If the church is not on earth at the time of the Great Tribulation, she cannot be on earth at the time of the Second Coming. *But, 2 Thessalonians 1 depicts the*

---

[21] Tim LaHaye and Thomas Ice, *Charting the End Times*, (Eugene, Ore, Harvest House, 2001)111. For a fuller discussion of the issue raised in this section, see my *Leaving The Rapture Behind*. (Ardmore, Ok. JaDon Productionsllc, 2004). Also, see my *We Shall Meet Him In The Air, the Wedding of the King of kings* for a full discussion of the entire rapture issue. This book is, to my knowledge, the first and only full preterist commentary ever written on 1 Thessalonians 4. It is available on Amazon, Kindle and my websites.

[22] Dwight Pentecost, *Things To Come*, (Grand Rapids, Zondervan, 1957)210.

church on earth, undergoing tribulation, at the time of the Second Coming.
Therefore, the millennial doctrine is wrong.

Some suggest that while the "true church" will not be on earth at the Second
Coming, *the apostate church* will be. This does not help. If 2 Thessalonians
addresses the apostate church experiencing the horrors of the Tribulation this
means that *Christ gives the apostate church relief from the Great Tribulation.* I
know of no millennialists that espouse this view.

2 Thessalonians 1 is speaking of the church under tribulation at the time of
the Second Coming. Since, patently, the church could not be under tribulation *in
heaven*, this means that she would have to be under tribulation on earth.
However, if the church is undergoing tribulation on earth at the time of the
Second Coming, then that has to be the *Great Tribulation*, according to the
millennialist. Since 2 Thessalonians depicts the church on earth at the time of the
Second Coming the millennial rapture doctrine is destroyed.

So, by positing 2 Thessalonians 1 as the Second Coming *the dispensationalist
has negated his entire doctrine.* 2 Thessalonians 1 cannot be speaking of the
rapture because it is the time of the judgment of the wicked. There is no place for
that in the millennial scheme. It cannot be speaking of the Second Coming
because it deals with the church and not Israel (2 Thessalonians 1:1). However,
if 2 Thessalonians 1 deals with the church then it cannot be speaking of the
Second Coming because according to the millennialists, the church is not on
earth at the *parousia*. If 2 Thessalonians 1 is speaking of the Second Coming and
it is dealing with giving the church relief from tribulation at that time, then
patently the church does go through the Great Tribulation after all. The church
is not raptured out before the Tribulation.

If the church is not on earth at the time of the Second Coming – having
been removed in the rapture–then how in the name of reason could Paul
promise that the church would be given relief from persecution (not
simply the stress of the human experience)– at the Second Coming?
This is a huge issue that Dispensationalists seldom, if ever, address.

Millennialists universally apply 2 Thessalonians 1 to the Second Coming, not the rapture. It is little wonder that in the millennial literature 2 Thessalonians 1 is barely discussed, and if it is discussed, it is moralized to teach that Christ will give his saints relief from the injustice of this life. But even *this* does not help since it still has the church on earth and delivered from trouble at the Second Coming.

Furthermore, if our conclusions here are correct, and it was to be Old Covenant Judah cast out of the presence of the Lord forever, then the dispensational doctrine is falsified. Paul said that the persecutors, i.e. *the Jews*, would be cast out of the presence of the Lord with "everlasting destruction." As suggested above, that hardly sounds like the national restoration of Israel demanded by the millennial doctrine. And what is so significant is that this casting out takes place at what the millennialists agree is the Second Coming. That means that instead of being nationally *restored* at Christ's Second Coming, Israel/ Judah was to be *destroyed*. This is *devastating* to the millennial view.

A FINAL THOUGHT:
HOW IS THIS POSSIBLE?

I will only mention this last point in passing since I have developed it extensively in my book *How Is This Possible?*[23] Here is the issue.

Let's say that the events of 2 Thessalonians 1 are to be understood literally, as all futurist eschatologies claim. Christ is to visibly, bodily, as a 5' 5" Jewish man, descend out of heaven, accompanied by the angels, while the entire cosmos goes up in flaming fire. At the same time, every human who has ever lived and died is reconstituted, restored to their body and raised out of the ground. And all of this takes place in the twinkling of an eye.

Well, if that is what the coming of the Lord is supposed to be, read 2 Thessalonians 2:1-2:

"Now, brethren, concerning the coming of our Lord Jesus Christ and our gathering together to Him, we ask you, not to be soon shaken in mind or troubled, either by spirit or by word or by letter, as if from us, as though the day of Christ **had come.** (my emphasis. And for the record, there is no doubt about the proper translation of the text. It is, "Don't let anyone deceive you into thinking that the Day of the Lord *has already come*").

Okay, so the coming of the Lord is an earth burning, time ending, cosmos destroying event, when every human corpse that has ever gone into the ground comes out. This is what I was raised believing, and what it still the dominant view (at least for the present time).

So, ask yourself the question: If the coming of the Lord is that literal, visible, physical event just described, how in the name of reason could the Thessalonians, or anyone else, believe it had already happened? Same goes for the popular concept of the resurrection. Some believed that event was also already past (2 Timothy 2:18).[24]

Could anyone convince you that the earth burned up yesterday? Could anyone convince you that every corpse of every human who had ever died had been raised out of the ground or the sea? Could anyone even begin to convince you that the Lord had visibly descended out of heaven in that 5'5" human body, when "every eye shall see him" and yet, you didn't?

---

[23] Don K. Preston, *How Is This Possible?* (Ardmore, Ok. 73401, JaDon Management Inc., 2009).

[24] See my book: *The Hymenaean Heresy: Reverse the Charges*, for a full discussion of the issue. Available from Amazon, Kindle, and my websites.

The problem here is real. Some at Thessalonica did believe the Lord had already come, in fulfillment of 2 Thessalonians 1! For the solution of how they could believe that, see my *How Is This Possible?* book.

Could anyone, convince anyone, that the coming of the Lord in 2 Thessalonians 1– *as traditionally interpreted* – had already happened? Such an idea is ludicrous in the extreme. Something else is clearly going on here, since some were believing that Christ had already come! Modern, orthodox Christianity simply has no answer for this conundrum, as is more than evident in the commentaries.

SUMMARY AND CONCLUSION

In this study we have demonstrated beyond doubt that 2 Thessalonians 1, cannot apply to any other event than the end of the Old Covenant Age of Israel in AD 70. With this demonstration we have thereby proven that all NT references to Christ's parousia predicted his coming at the end of the Old Covenant Age of Israel in AD 70. This is true because 2 Thessalonians 1 predicted the same thing as Acts 1, 1 Corinthians 15, 1 Thessalonians 4:13f, etc..

We have shown definitively that 2 Thessalonians 1 was a prophecy of the consummation of Israel's last days.

We have shown that 2 Thessalonians quotes *verbatim* from Isaiah 2 and that Jesus applies the very same verses to his coming in judgment of Jerusalem for shedding his blood.

We have shown that 2 Thessalonians 1 is perfectly consistent with Jesus' prediction of coming judgment on Israel for her long history of persecuting the saints. 2 Thessalonians 1 is but a reiteration, in graphic form, of Matthew 23:29f.

We have shown that the consistent application of Isaiah, by Jesus, Paul and John, is to the AD 70 judgment coming of Jesus Christ.

We have shown that Paul's promise of relief from persecution was made to living breathing human beings being persecuted for their faith.

We have shown that Paul promised those living humans that their relief from that persecution would be "when the Lord Jesus is revealed from heaven."

We have shown that Paul was not saying that the Thessalonians would die to receive their desired relief.

We have shown that Paul was not saying that the Thessalonians would go to Abraham's bosom to receive their relief.

We have shown that Paul's statement that the persecutors would be cast out of the presence of the Lord demands that he is speaking of Old Covenant Judah. No other people had dwelt in His presence. No other people could be cast out of His presence.

We have shown that the relief from their persecution would be "when the Lord Jesus is revealed from heaven." This *demands* that the *Thessalonians*, not American Christians, or Nigerian Christians, or Russian Christians, *but the first century Thessalonian Christians* had to be enduring persecution at the time of the parousia, for it was to be the parousia of Christ that was to give them relief from that persecution.

We have shown that if Paul's promise/prophecy was not fulfilled in the lifetime of the Thessalonians, giving them relief from their persecution, then Paul is revealed as a false prophet.

36

We have shown that to turn Thessalonians into a prediction of a yet future, end of time coming of Christ, that *you have to ignore everything that is said in the text.* You have to ignore, or alter, the identity of those to whom the book was written. You have to ignore what was happening to them at the time. You have to ignore what Paul was promising them, relief from that present persecution. You have to ignore who it was that was persecuting them. You have to ignore the prophetic source of the prophecy which proves that Paul did not have a visible, bodily coming of Christ in mind. You essentially have to say that the epistle to the church of God at Thessalonica, written 2000 years ago, *had no relevance whatsoever to the very people to whom it was addressed.*

To apply 2 Thessalonians 1 to a future coming of the Lord, is to say that the epistle addressed to the church of God at Thessalonica, written 2000 years ago, *had no relevance whatsoever to the very people to whom it was addressed.* This would be like saying you received a letter addressed to you from the IRS, promising you relief from all tax liability. Yet, when you tried to take advantage of that, the IRS tells you that the letter has nothing to do with you, but some generation of citizens 2000 years in the future!

In other words, in order to turn 2 Thessalonians 1:4f into a prediction of a yet future coming of the Lord, *you have to ignore or distort every known rule of proper interpretation.* Isn't that a bit dangerous?

We have shown that just as 2 Thessalonians 1 foretold, the Lord Jesus was revealed from heaven in AD 70. He came in the same manner that his Father had come many times in the OT. He came in judgment of the persecutors of the Thessalonians, i.e. Old Covenant Judah. He came and gave the Thessalonians relief from their persecution. Paul was not wrong, he was not deluded. He was *inspired* and the Bible text is completely trustworthy.